BREAK OUT

NO WARNING SHOTS FIRED

SAN QUENTIN PRISON COLLECTIVE

ISBN 978-1-938901-99-7

Copyright © 2018, 2019, 2020

All rights reserved. Printed in the United States of America.

The San Quentin Graphic Novel Collective

Break Out is a collection of short comics created by artists in the California State Prison, San Quentin's Arts in Corrections program. It was inspired by a beloved teacher, Rene Garcia, and facilitated by Sonia Wallach with the support of the William James Association.

San Quentin Prison Arts Project, William James Association would like to thank:

- Arts in Corrections: A program of the California Department of Corrections & Rehabilitation and California Arts Council
- Ron Davis, warden, San Quentin State Prison (SQSP)
- Lt. Sam Robinson, public information officer, SQSP
- Steven Emrick, community partnerships manager, SQSP

CONTENTS

Angry Man, by F. Tinsley — 3

Me, by M. Stanley — 11

Hijinks and Hightail, by P. Stauffer — 18

Doors of Dementia, by O. Smith — 28

War, by B. Richie — 32

Jack, by B. Fowler — 39

Park, Zoo, Beach, by G. Harrell — 48

Black Wolf, by L. Padgett — 54

Scab & Dusty, by J. Craft — 61

Tah Sue, by C. Bun — 68

Some Fun, by B. Chandler — 76

G-Mo & Loom, by N. C. Bucci — 84

Cult of the Piranha, by O. Smith — 92

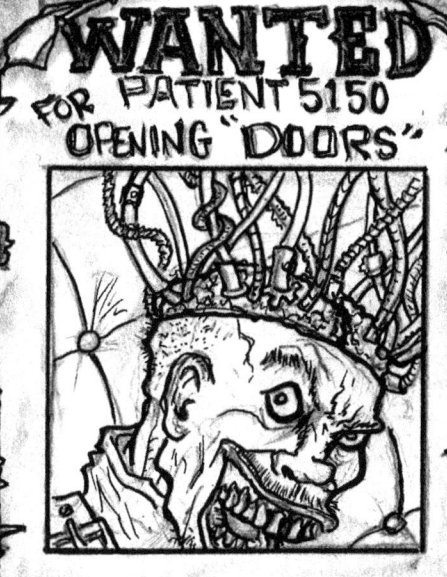

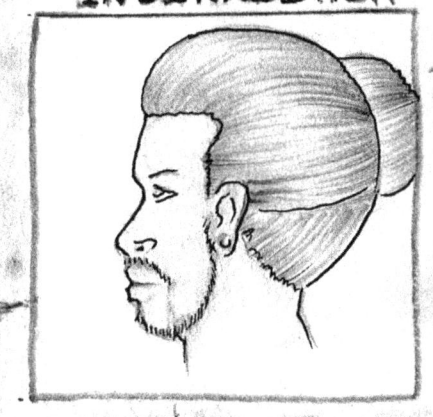
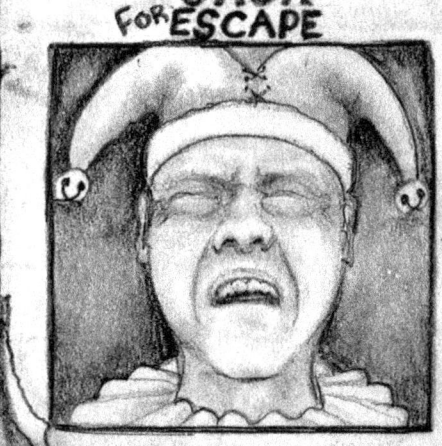

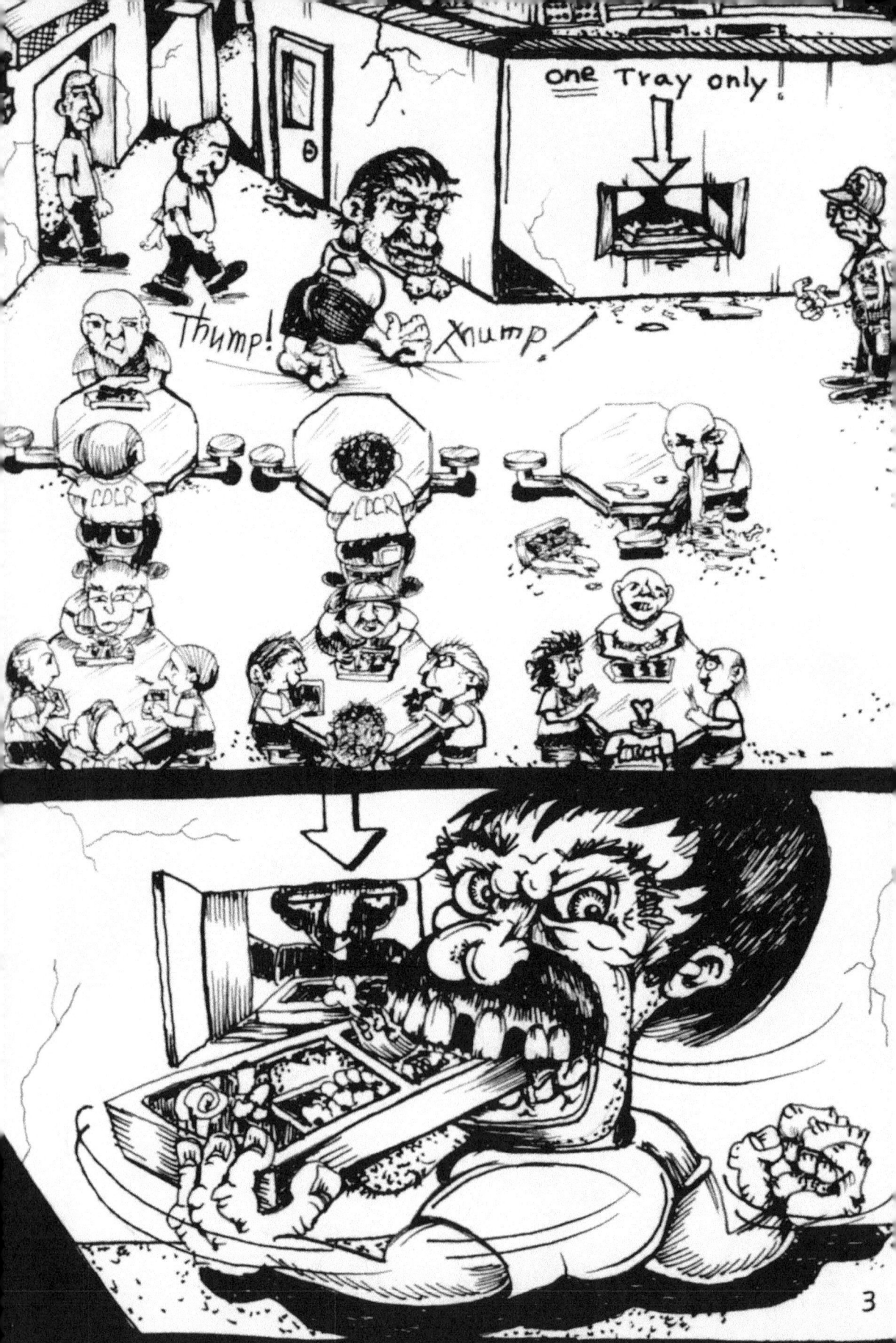

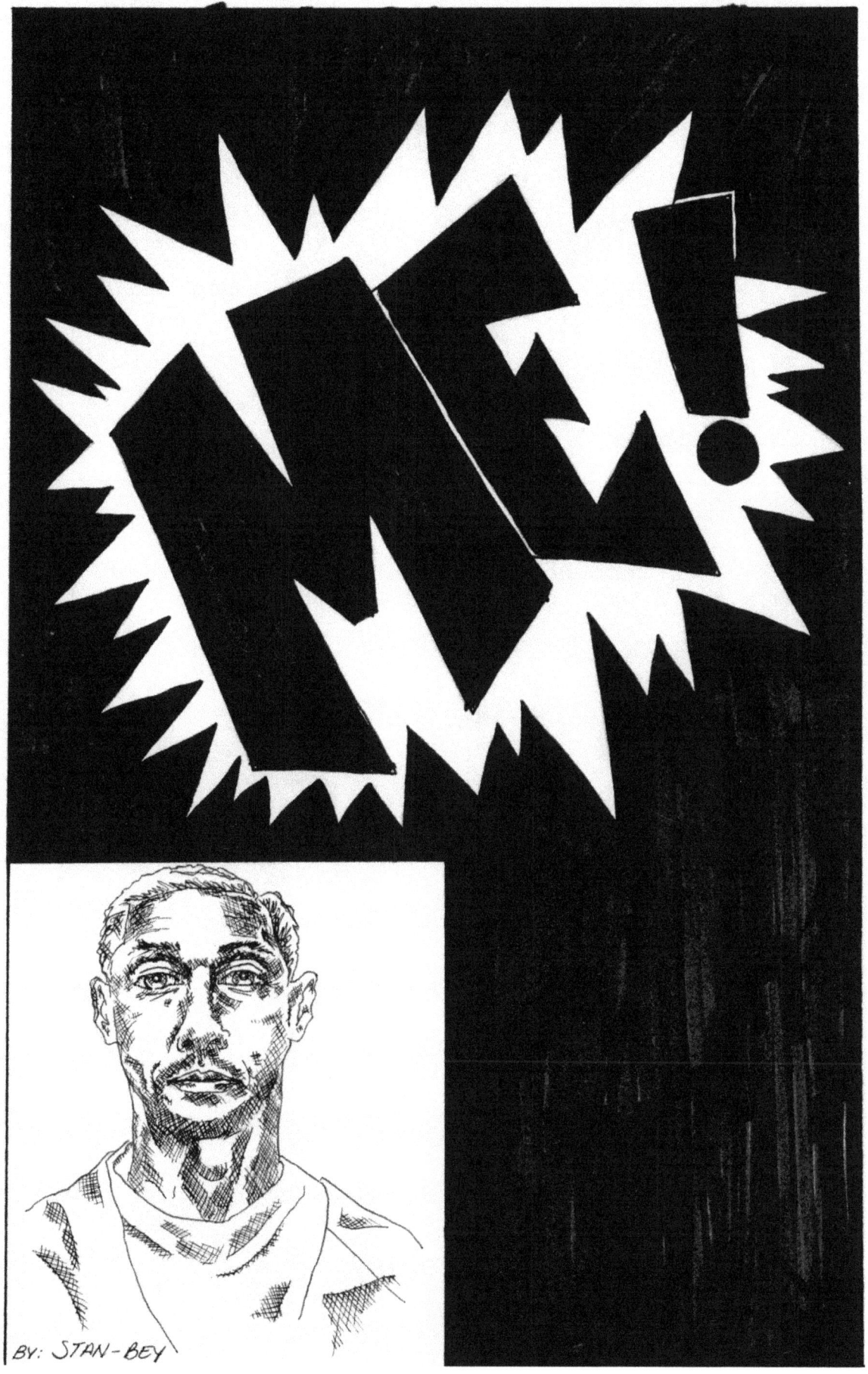

SO... ME HAS RECEIVED A BODY. WHATS TO BECOME OF ME, NOW... ...BASED ON HIS CHOICE?
NOTICE! THERES NO STATEMENT FROM SUNLIGHT. INTERESTING, INDEED!

TO BE CONTINUED...

HiJinx & HiTail

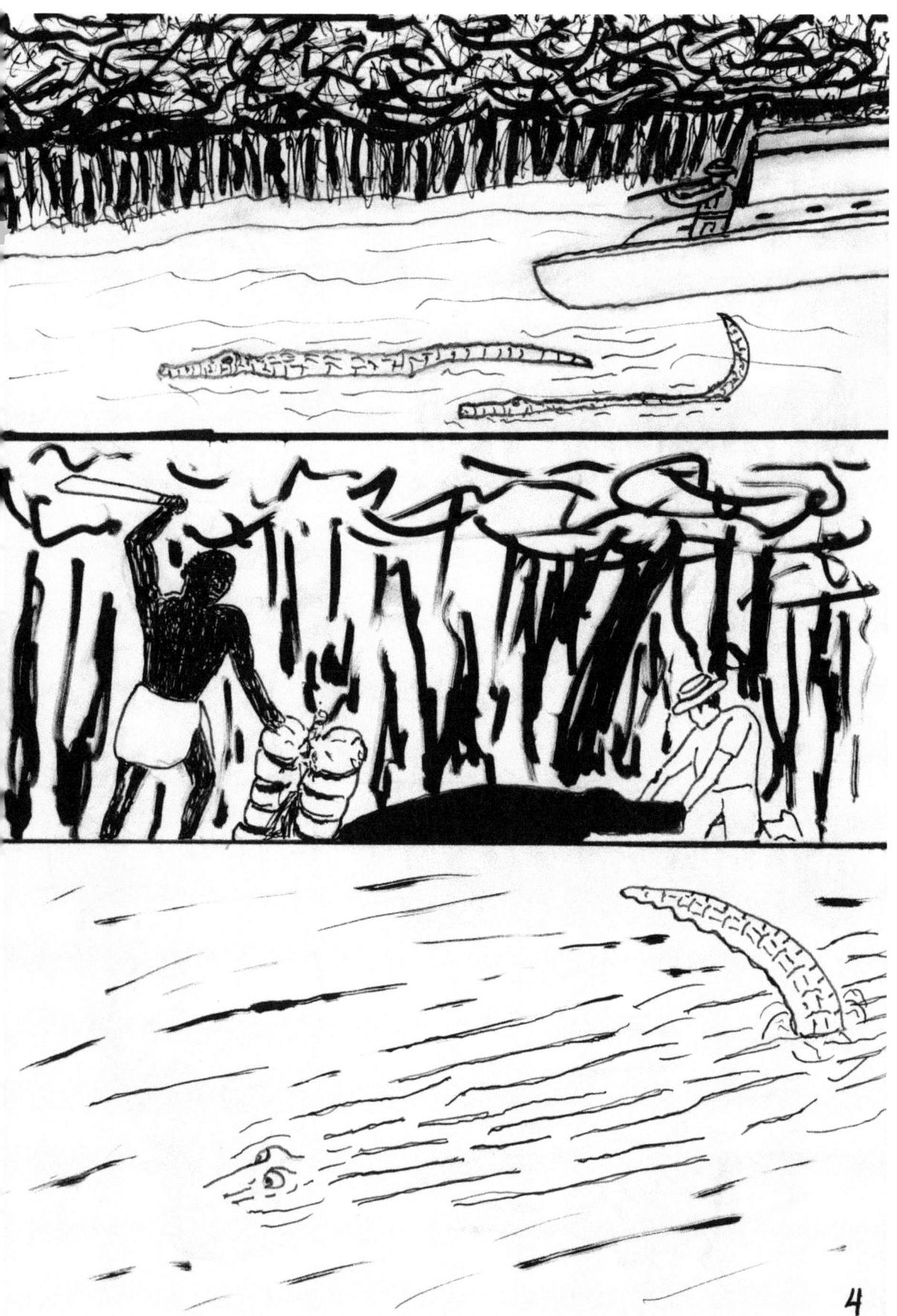

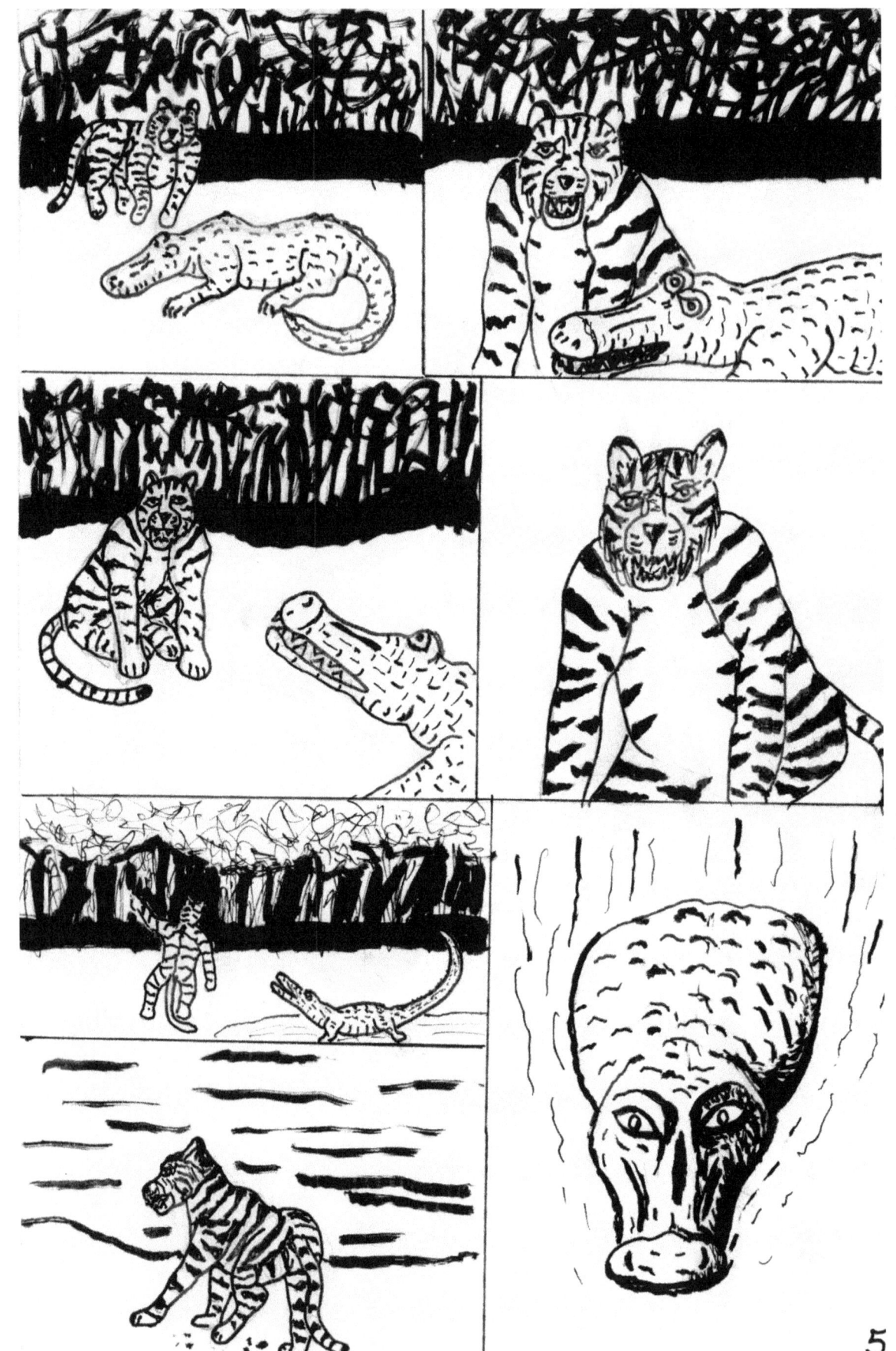

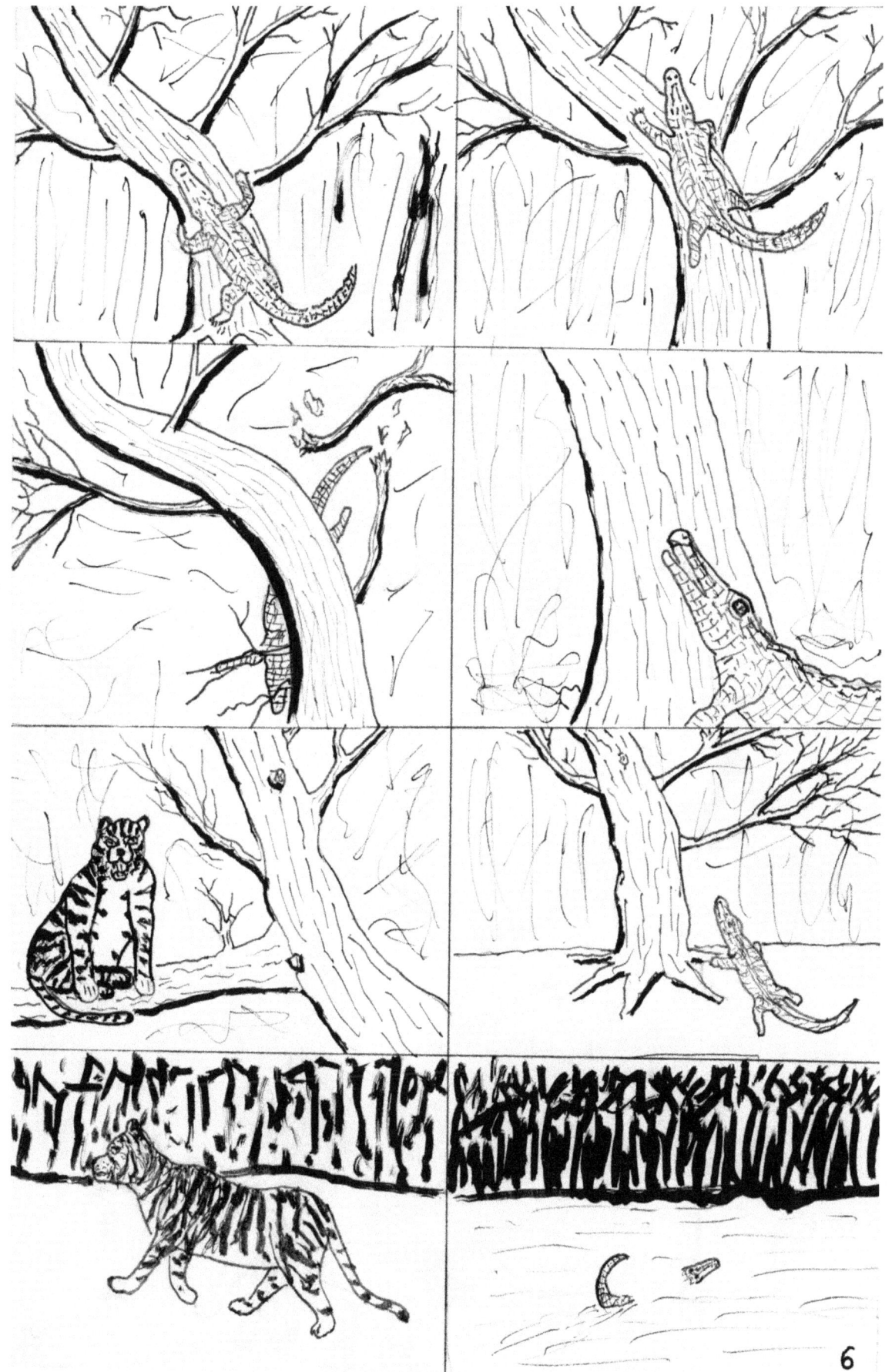

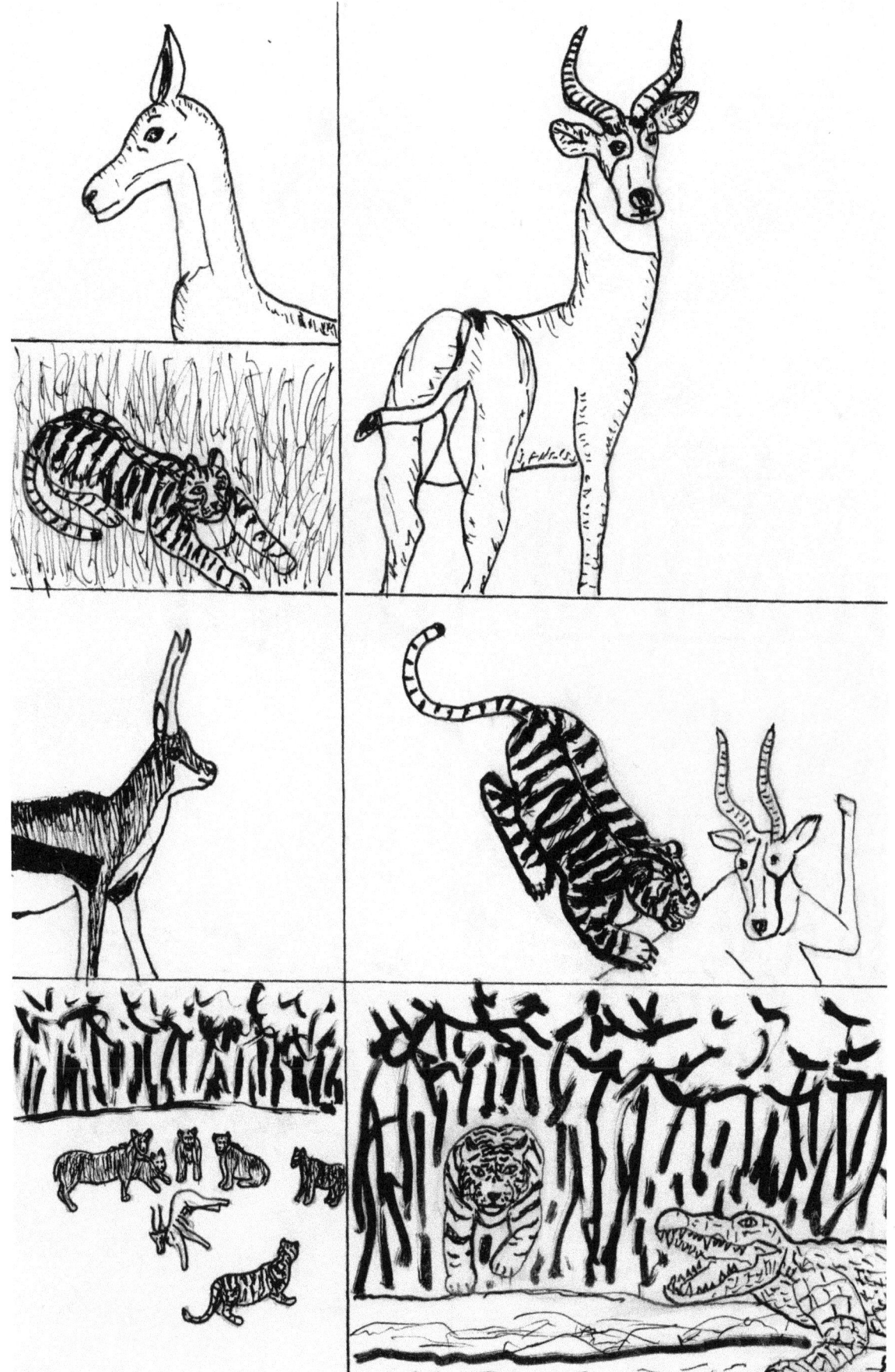

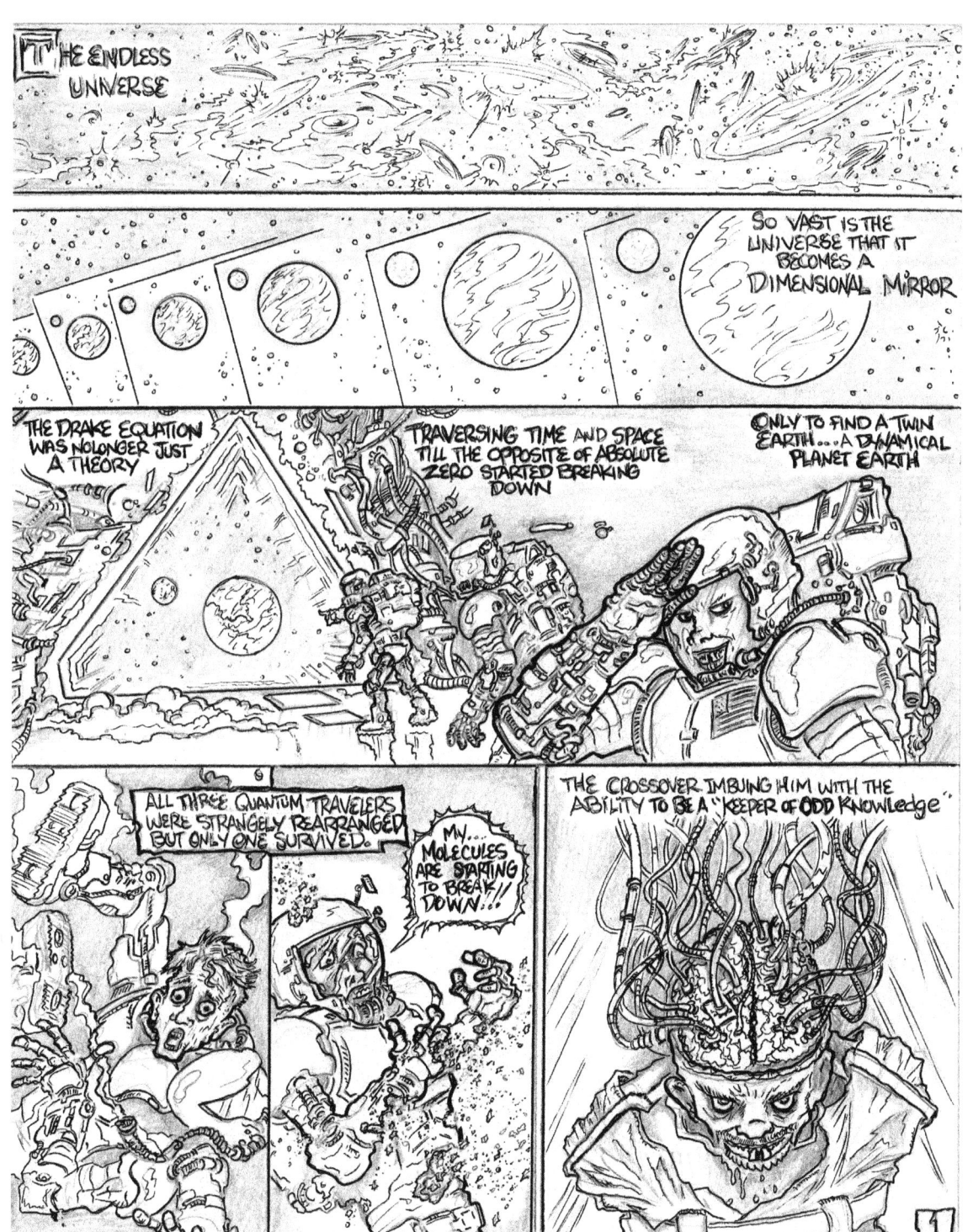

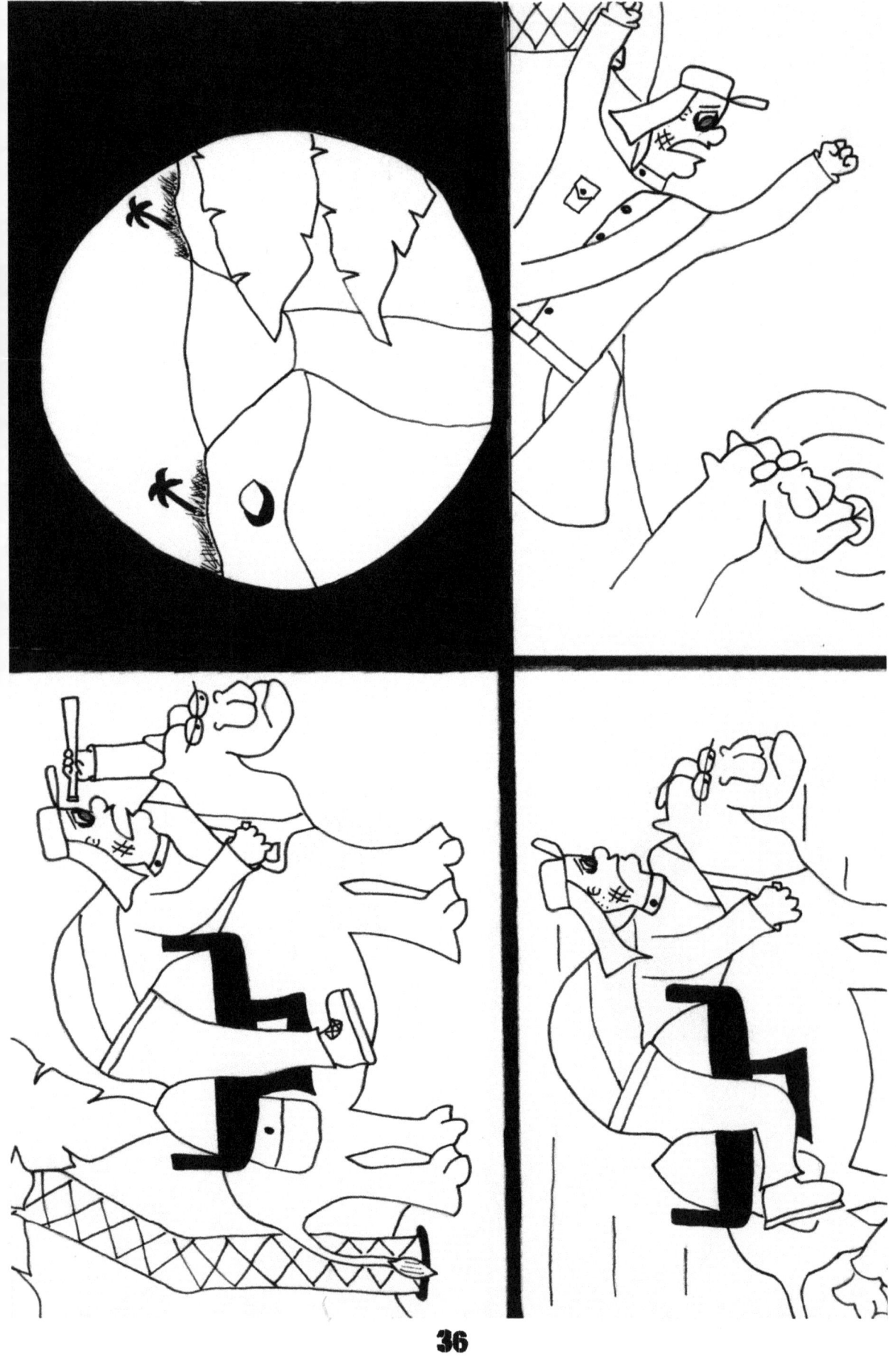

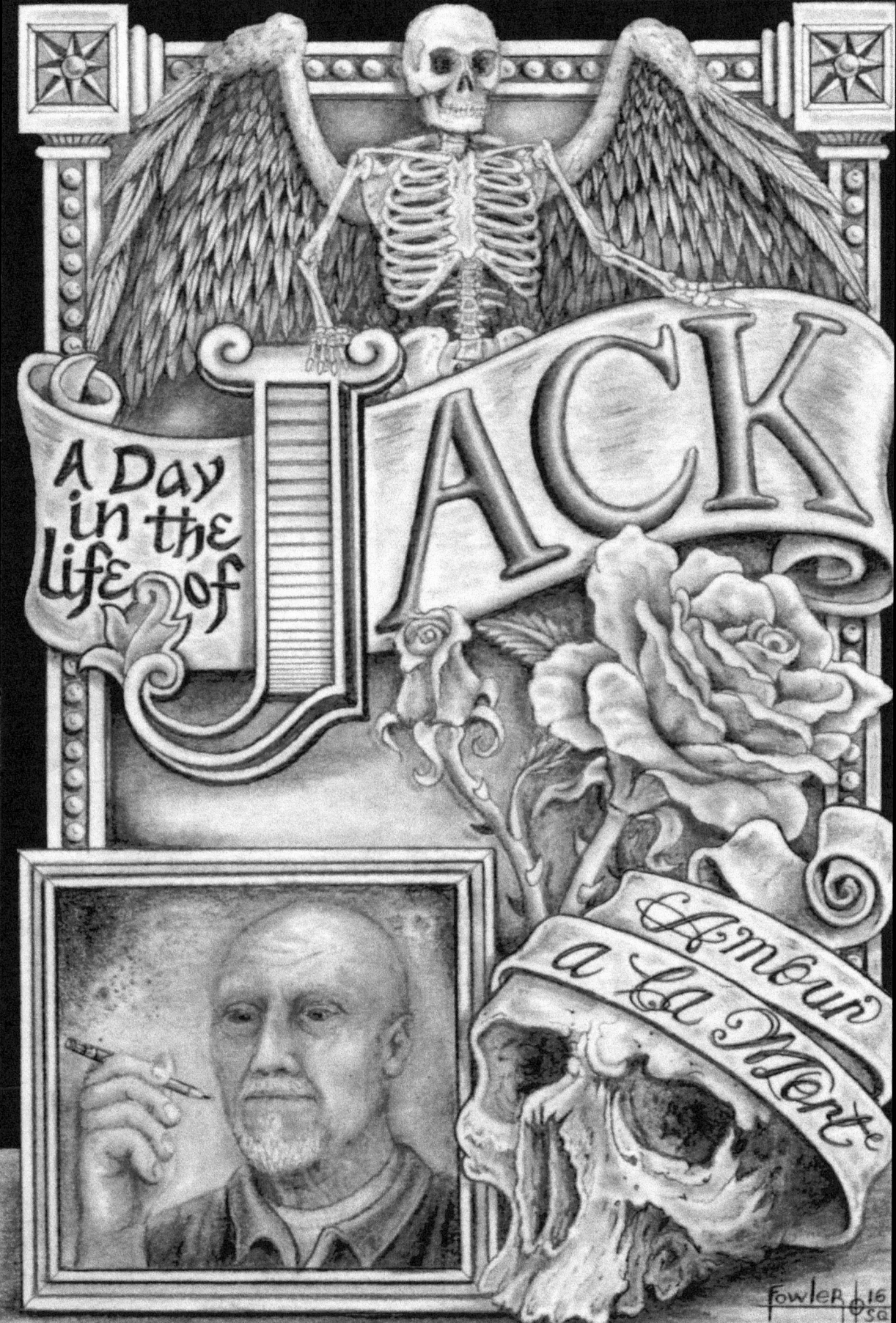

In This House Two Kinders Born Where Once Was Four Ones Left To Mourn.

Heed My Advice Tread Not Inside For Specters Dwell of Those Who've Died.

So Long Ago In Salad Days Young Lovers Kissed And Children Played

Thorns Draw Blood While Roses Bloom As Bad And Good Live In This Room.

—A Slice Of Heaven That Went To Hell, A Painful Story These Walls Could Tell.

One Left Behind He Knows Not Why To Figure Out He'll Try And Try...

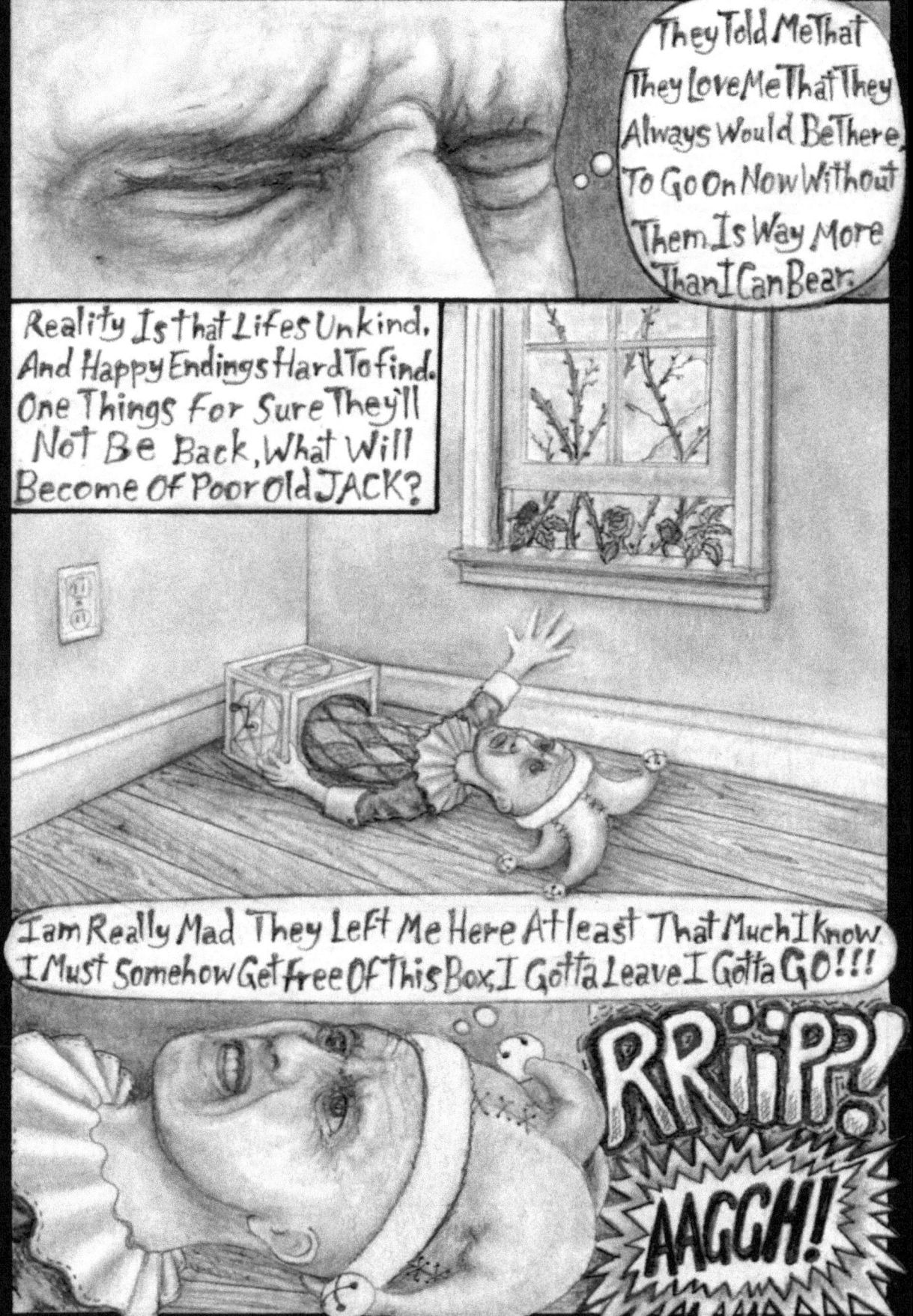

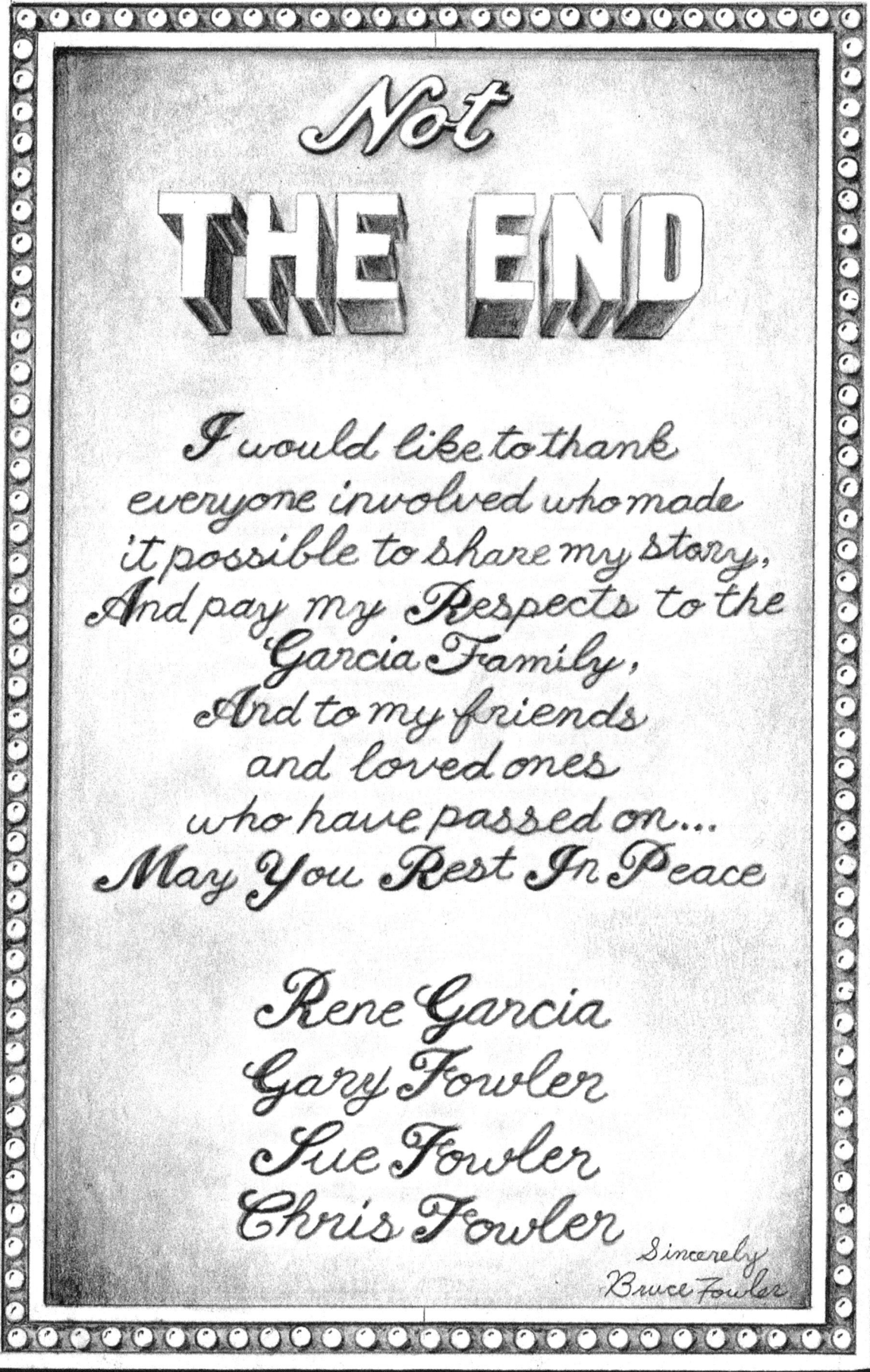

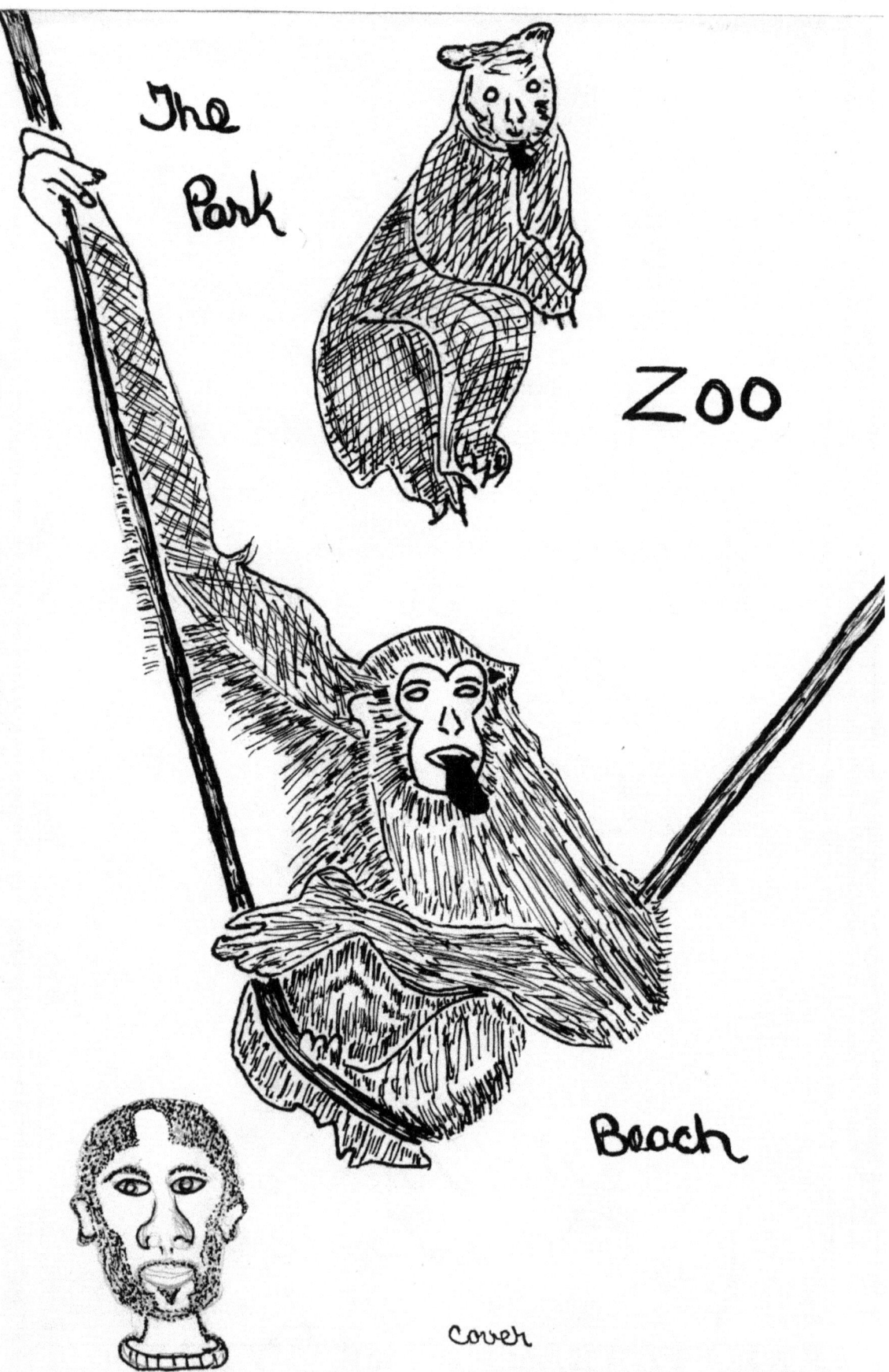

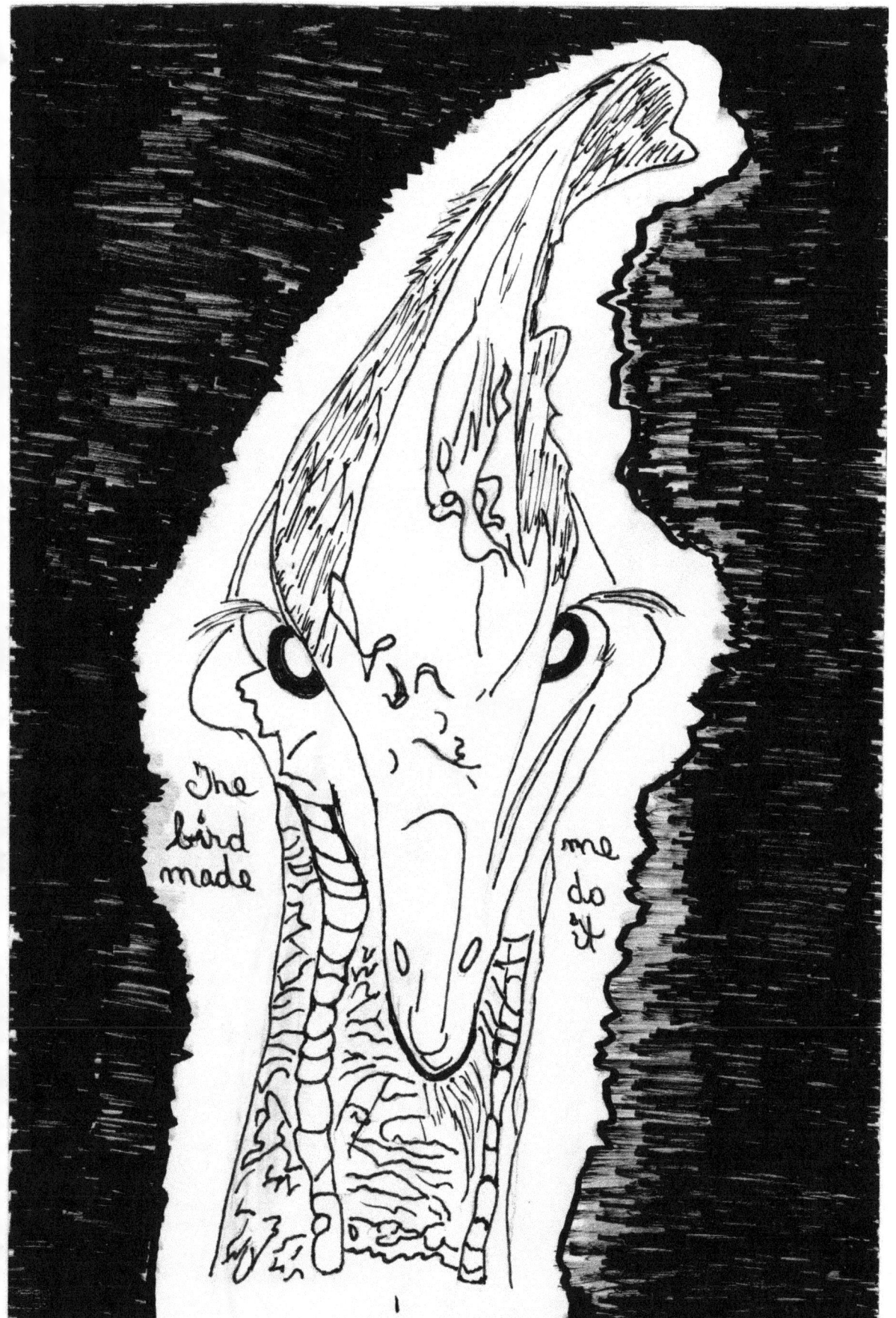

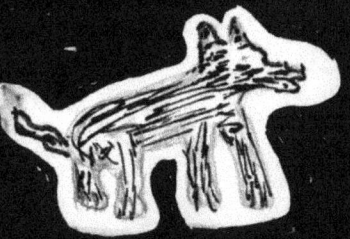

nothing but

The dog

In me

Sam never takes

me any where

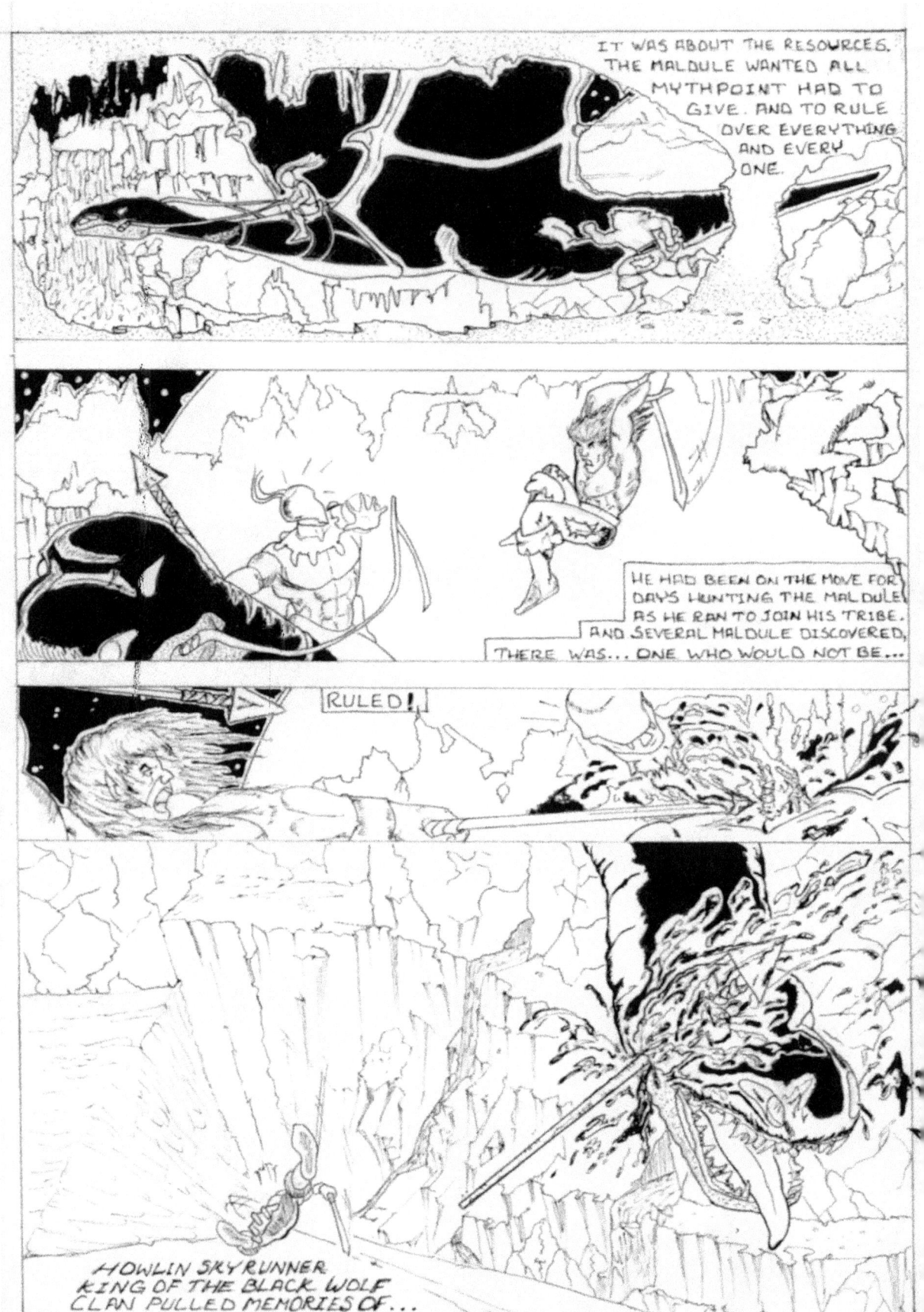

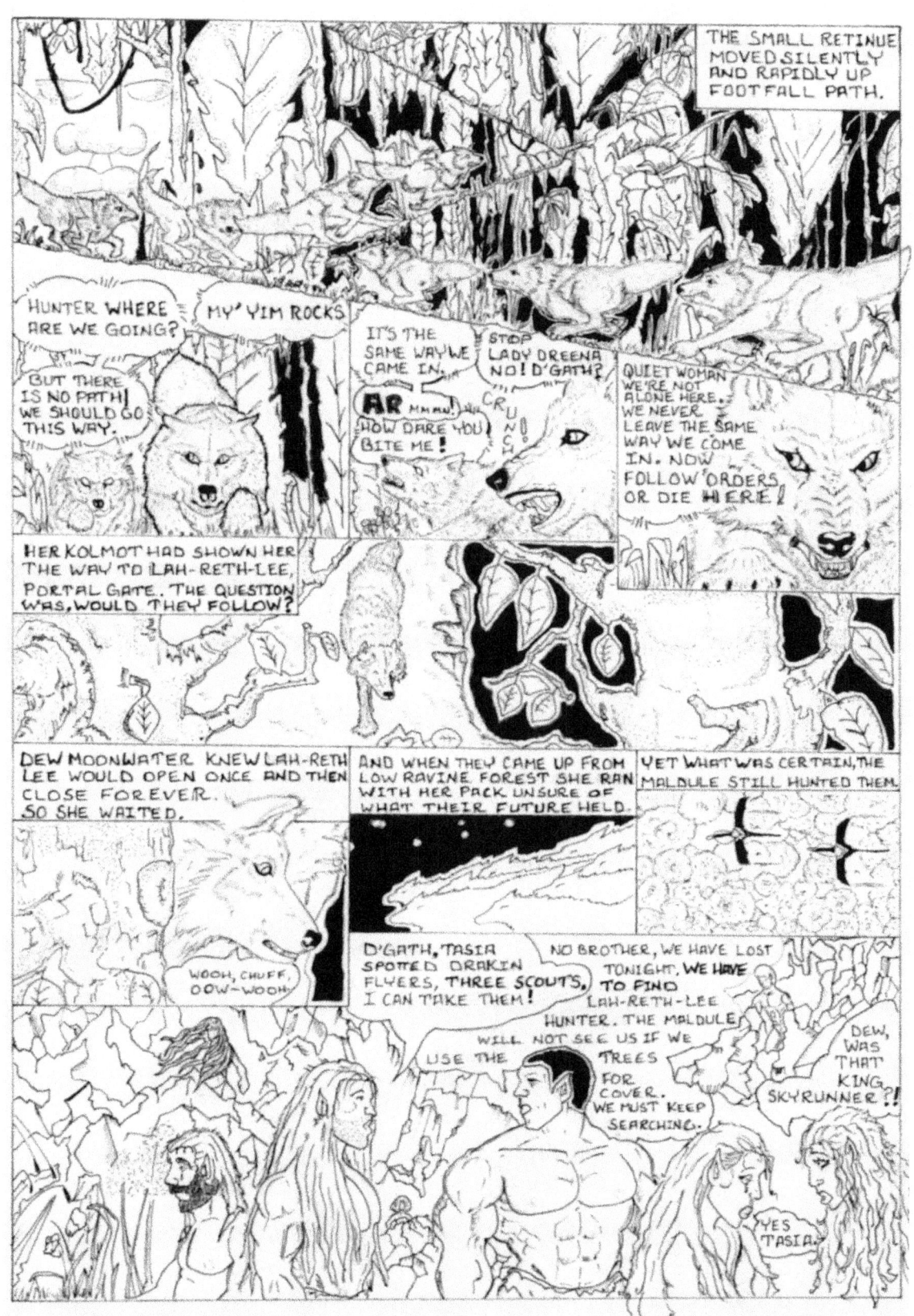

AFTER A GREAT WAR, KING ANGKRAMAN UNITED ALL THE LANDS, PEACE AND PROSPERITY FLORISHED.

UPON THE KING'S DEATH, PRINCE ANGKRABONG WAS BETRAYED BY THE TENTH QUEEN ANGKRAJUHT SO THAT HER SON PRINCE ANGKRAPOM, SECOND IN LINE TO THE THRONE, CAN BECOME KING.

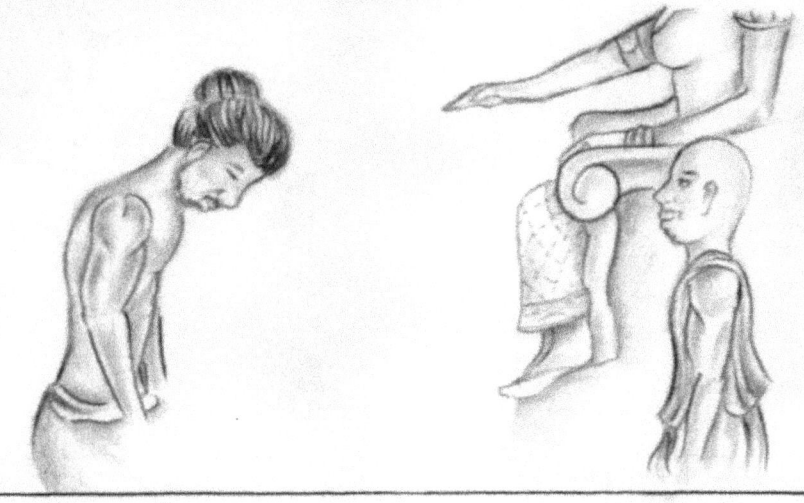

THE ASSASSIN WAS LOYAL TO THE KING AND COULD NOT CARRY OUT HIS MISSION. TO SAVE THE KING, HIS MOTHER TOOK HER OWN LIFE.

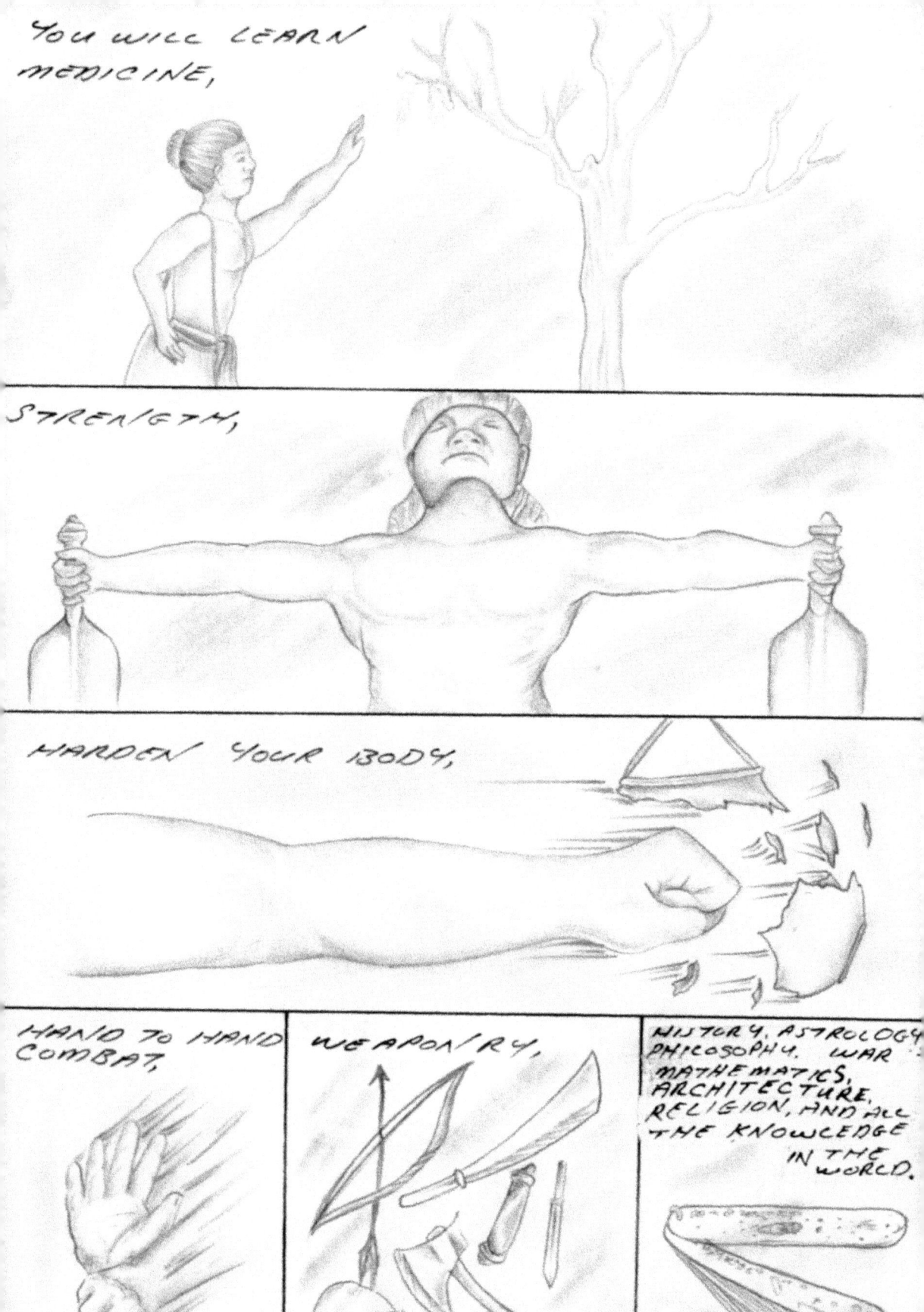

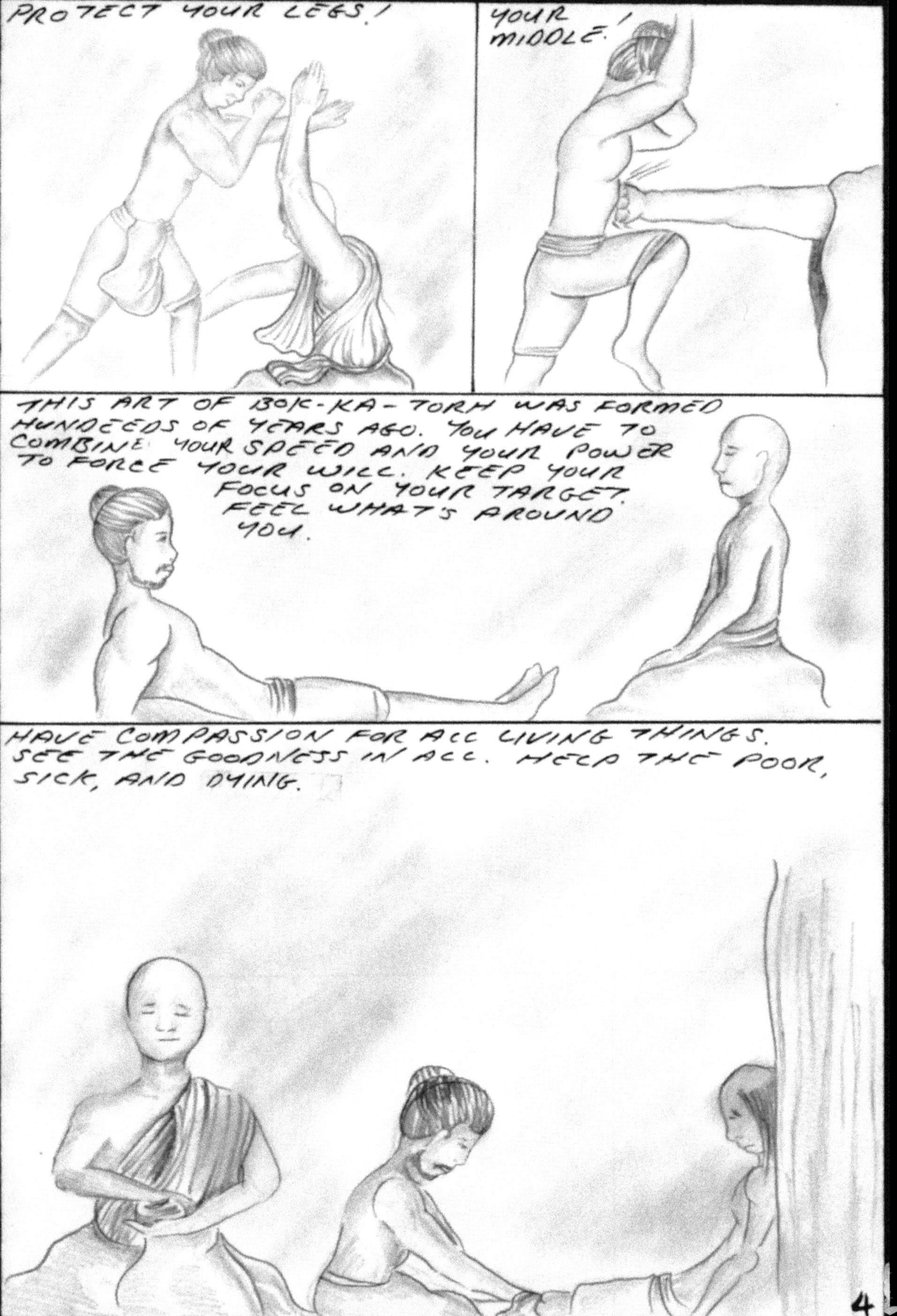

Sok, you are now a Kruh. I have given you all of me and my line. You are now the line. I have only one more thing to teach you.

What is it Lok-Kruh?

You. Me?

Sok, your true name is Ankrabong. You are the rightful king of Angkra. King Angkrapoh is your young brother. He knows nothing of you. He is under Queen Angkrapakih's spell. She and her Kruh rule the kingdom this way.

Upon your father's death, Queen Angkrapakih order me to assassinate you and your mother. Your father before his death ordered and pledged me to look over you and protect you with my life.

Your mother took her own life so you can live.

MY KING, YOUR KINGDOM..

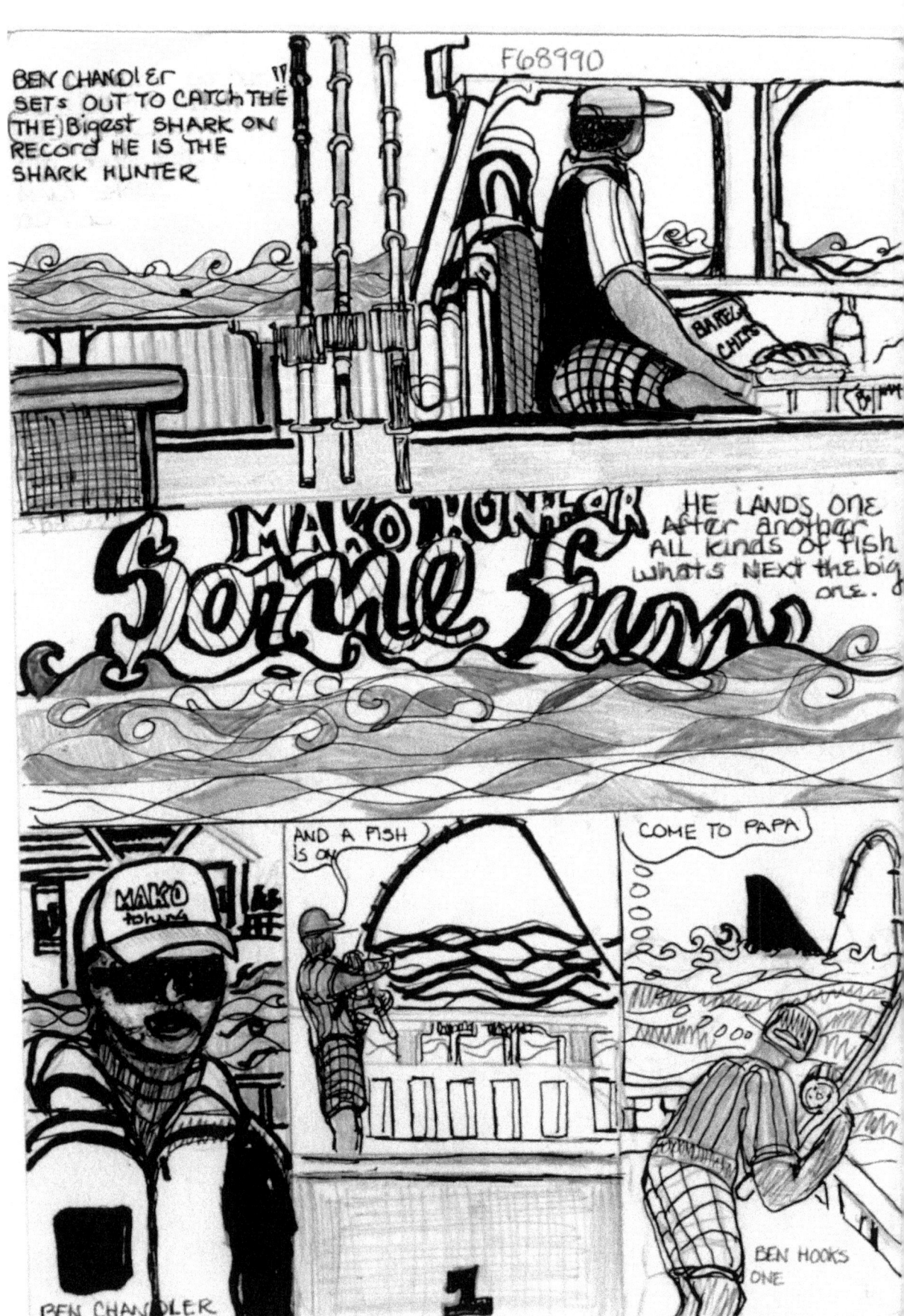

TAKE YOUR KiDS Fishing

BEN CHANDLER is one off from being a perfect Dad!! The one is one more kid. fishing is our was his life. i think he might stay home and fish for sun fish with his kids now.

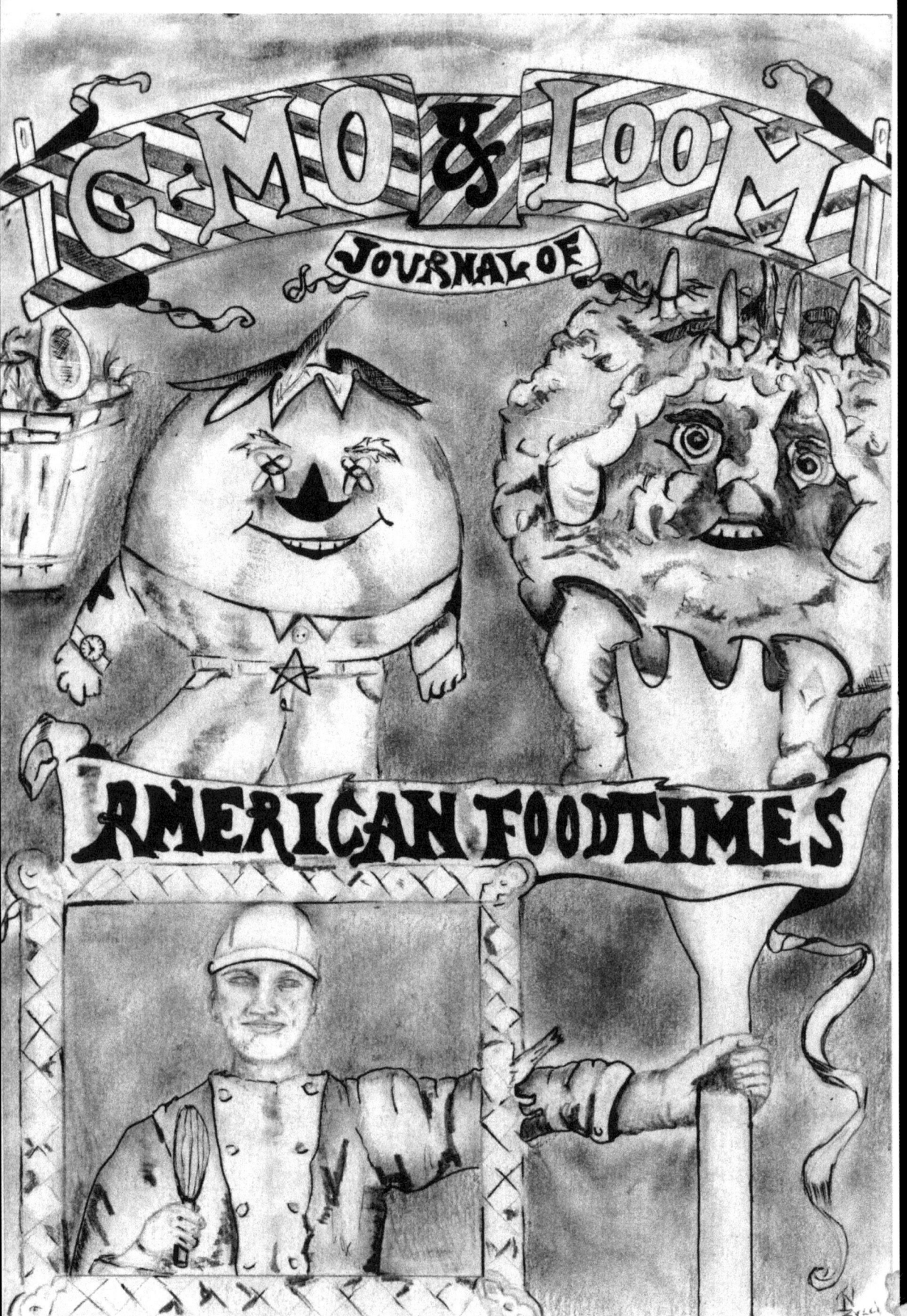

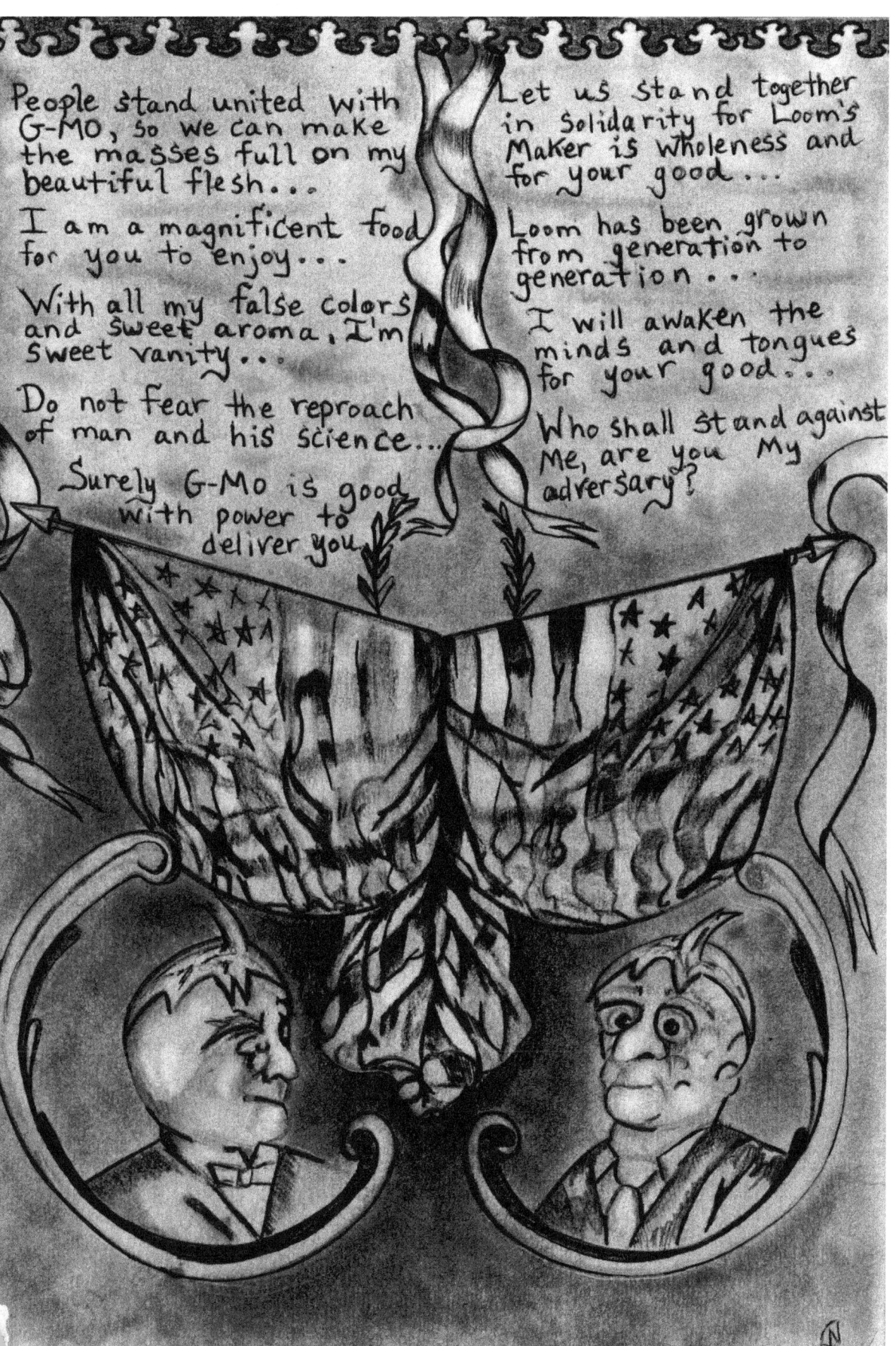

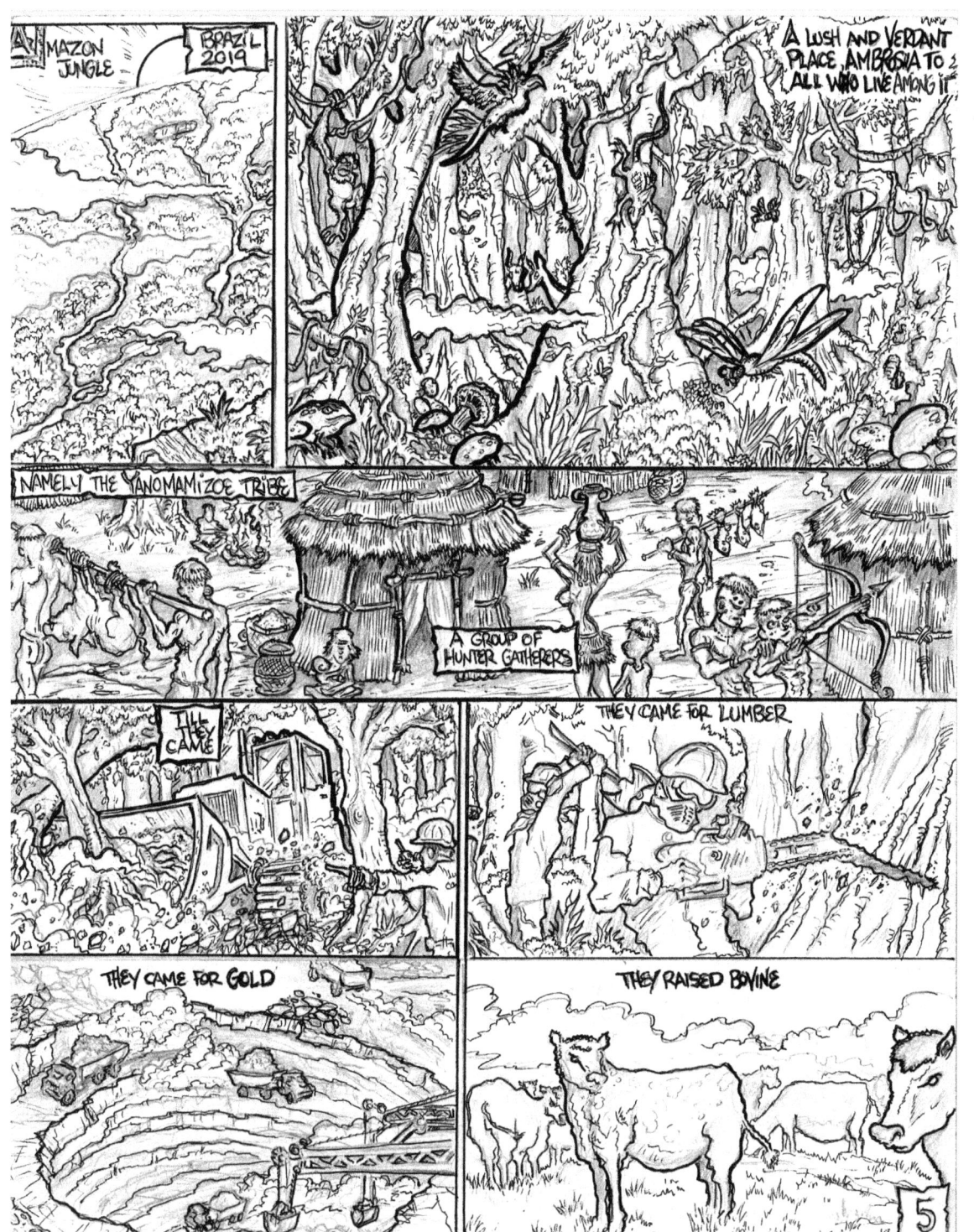

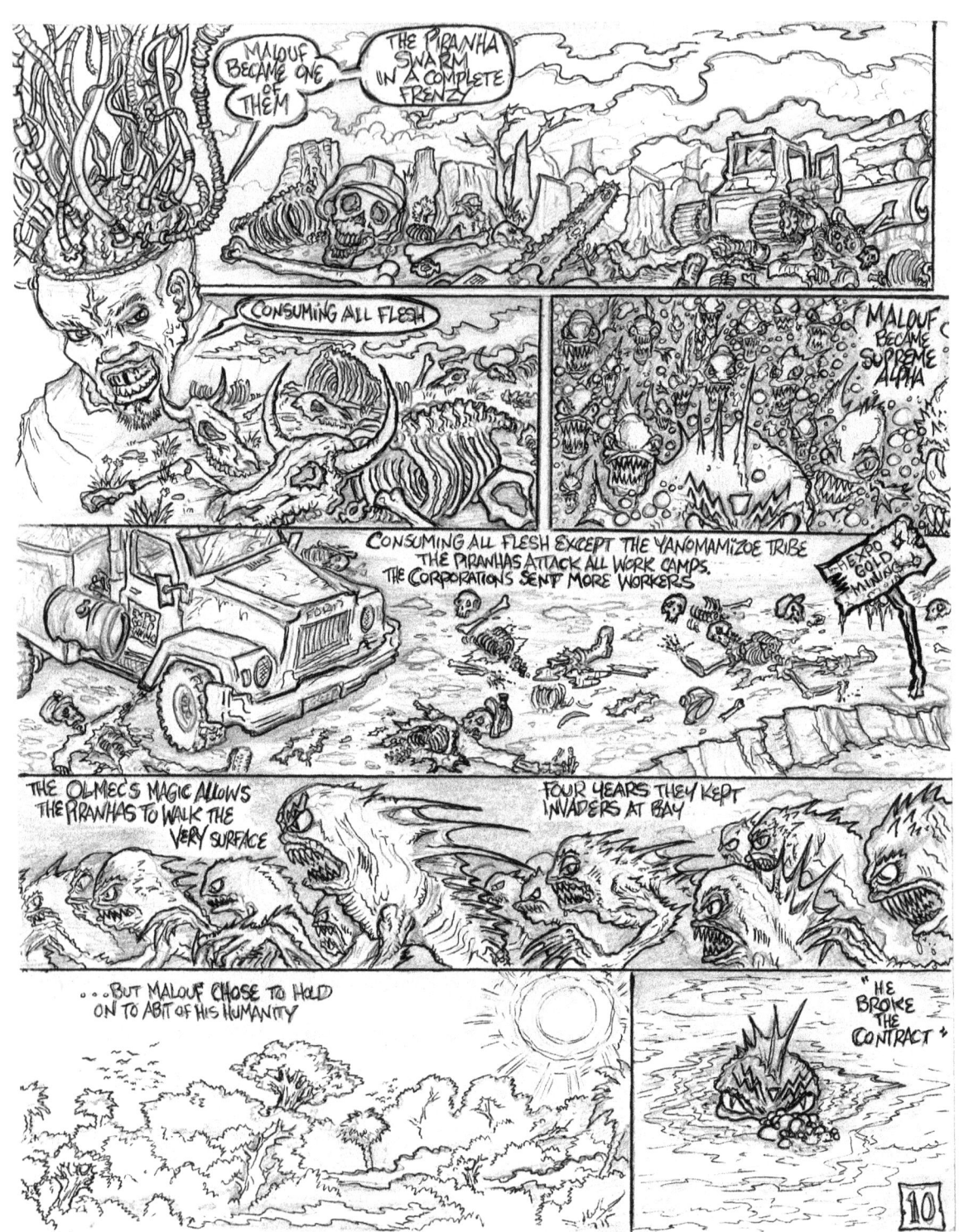

www.ingramcontent.com/pod-product-compliance
Lightning Source LLC
Chambersburg PA
CBHW081200020426
42333CB00020B/2584